ENRY

JAMES

PERCY

MEET ALL THESE FRIENDS IN BUZZ BOOKS:

Thomas the Tank Engine
The Animals of Farthing Wood
Biker Mice From Mars
James Bond Junior
Fireman Sam
Joshua Jones
Rupert
Babar

First published 1992 by Buzz Books
an imprint of Reed Children's Books
Michelin House, 81 Fulham Road, London SW3 6RB
and Auckland, Melbourne, Singapore and Toronto

Reprinted 1993 (Twice)

Copyright © William Heinemann Ltd 1992

All publishing rights: William Heinemann Ltd
All television and merchandising rights licensed by
William Heinemann Ltd to Britt Allcroft (Thomas) Ltd
exclusively, worldwide

Photographs © Britt Allcroft (Thomas) Ltd 1992
Photographs by David Mitton and Terry Permane
for Britt Allcroft's production of Thomas the Tank
Engine and Friends

ISBN 185591 249 X

Printed and bound in Italy by Olivotto

NO JOKE FOR JAMES

buzz books

James is a mixed traffic engine. He can pull both trucks and coaches. He is proud of his smart red paint and so is his driver.

"Everyone says you brighten up their day, James."

One morning, James whistled loudly at the other engines.

"Look at me. I am the smartest, most useful engine on the line."

"Rubbish," replied Thomas. "We're all useful. The Fat Controller says so and he's Sir Topham Hatt, head of the whole railway."

"You know what, James?" added Percy.
"What?" replied James.
"You're getting all puffed up!"
James huffed away.

Later he was still boasting. "I'm the pride of the line."

"I saw you pulling trucks today. You're only a goods engine!" snorted Gordon.

James was furious. "I pull coaches too!"

"Not as much as I do," grunted Gordon.

"But the Fat Controller has plans for me."

James was only making this up, but Gordon believed him.

"What plans?"

"Er - wait and see."

"Oh dear," thought James. "Now what'll I do?"

Thomas was shunting shining new coaches.

"Good morning, James."

"Are those coaches for me?" asked James hopefully.

"No. These are for Gordon's express. I'll fetch your trucks next."

But James was going to play a trick on the other engines.

"Actually Thomas, I'm taking the coaches. The Fat Controller asked me to tell you."

"What about the trucks?"

"Er - give them to Gordon."

"Come on, Thomas," said his driver.
"Orders are orders."

So when James's driver returned, James
was coupled to the coaches and he puffed
away.

Thomas returned with the trucks. A few minutes later Gordon arrived.

"Where's the express?"

Thomas told him about James.

"And so here are your trucks."

Gordon was very cross and so was his
driver.

"Wait till the Fat Controller hears about this!"

Meanwhile, James was enjoying himself enormously.

"What a clever plan, what a clever plan," he chuffed.

Then he saw the Fat Controller.

"Some jokes are funny, but not this
one, James. You have caused confusion."

"Yes, Sir," said James.

"You will stay in your shed until you
are wanted."

The other engines teased James.

"I wonder who'll be pulling the express today?" said Gordon.

"I expect it'll be you," replied Henry.
"James is stuck in the shed for being silly!"
James felt sad.

Next morning, he went back to work.

"Hello," whistled Thomas. "Good to see you out and about again."

"I'm sorry I tricked you," said James.
"Are these my trucks?"

"Yes," replied Thomas kindly. "They are
pleased to have you back."

James puffed into the harbour with his goods train of trucks. He bustled about all day, pushing and pulling them into place.

"Time to go home now, James," said his driver at last. "No trucks or passengers, just we two."

But his driver was wrong.

"Excuse me," called a man. "I have a meeting with Sir Topham Hatt and I mustn't be late. May I ride back with you?"

"Of course," replied James's driver. Then he whispered to James, "This gentleman is a railway inspector."

James was most impressed. He steamed along the line as smoothly and quickly as he could.

The Fat Controller was waiting and the railway inspector greeted him warmly.

"This clever engine gave me a splendid ride. You must be proud of him."

"Yes indeed. James, once again you *are* a Really Useful Engine."

THOMAS

EDWARD

GORDON